CHURCH Hurt Healed ME

Tammy J. Carpenter

Church Hurt Healed Me
Copyright © 2019 by Tammy J. Carpenter

ISBN: 978-0997535846

Published by Effectual Concepts LLC
Greenville, South Carolina

Cover Design by Unveiled Creations - Greer, South Carolina

All rights reserved. Printed in the United States of America
No part of this book may be reproduced or used in any manner
without the express written permission of the publisher except
for the use of brief quotations in a book review.

Unless otherwise noted, all scripture quotations are from the
New American Standard Bible.

DEDICATION

This book is for us;
the church;
the body of Christ.
With love.

[15]but speaking the truth in love, we are to grow up in all aspects into Him who is the head, even Christ, [16]from whom the whole body, being fitted and held together by what every joint supplies, according to the proper working of each individual part, causes the growth of the body for the building up of itself in love.
                                    -Ephesians 4:15, 16

TABLE OF CONTENTS

Chapter 1:
The Church *1*

Chapter 2:
My Experience *5*

Chapter 3:
Prone To Injury *11*

Chapter 4:
The Wound *17*

Chapter 5:
The Infection *27*

Chapter 6:
The Handicap *35*

Chapter 7:
Not Just A "Church Girl" *41*

Chapter 8:
Your Personal Check Up *47*

About The Author *53*

CHAPTER 1

THE CHURCH

―――

There are many perspectives on the relevance and purpose of the church; especially considering the way it has evolved. In the right company, we could easily involve ourselves in a debate about the church's role. The size of the congregation, who the leader is, how often we attend, or is it even necessary to attend are a few of the topics that could spark controversial conversation. What's not up for debate, however, is God's love and His plan for us. His love yielded a plan of redemption that offers infallible truth to those that receive it.

This is not intended to be an exhaustive teaching on the church, but I will briefly expound on a passage in Matthew 16 when Jesus says, *"...and upon this rock I will build My church; and the gates of Hades will not overpower it."* Matthew 16:18

When I read that passage, it speaks to God's purpose for the church. Let's break it down for understanding:

Upon this rock: Rocks are foundational materials. They are typically hard stones and used to build or construct a firm foundation or support. Based on Peter's confession of who Christ is, a foundation is established.

I will build My church: This statement shows Christ's declaration of participation in the construction, shaping and molding of His church. In this particular passage, Jesus is speaking and He intentionally uses the phrase, "My church," which makes it clear that the desire for a church was not man made.

Gates of Hades will not overpower it: This signifies declared protection, stability and victory. God covers what belongs to Him.

There are many passages that reference or mention the church in The Bible. The church is a necessary and intentional organization; intentional in that the church has a purpose and serves a purpose. The church is also known as the body of Christ. 1 Corinthians 12:27 states, *"Now ye are the body of Christ, and members in particular."* Therefore, as Christians, we are a part of the church as a whole, even if we don't associate with a specific denomination or local church.

As vital as the church is, it has been misunderstood and mishandled by many. This shouldn't be as alarming as we make it. We are imperfect people, and things we are attached to, things we create and oversee, will also have imperfections. Oftentimes when issues or imperfections surface from an individual that's a member of the church, it unfortunately becomes an indictment against the church as a whole. We, as "church people," tend to be so unforgiving. I purposely said "we" because I am included in those that need grace daily, but have failed to extend it and empathize with others.

I'm so grateful for God's grace! I'm overwhelmed by His unfailing love! In spite of us and our flaws, it's God's love and grace that works through broken vessels to continue to touch and transform lives through the church.

CHAPTER 2

MY EXPERIENCE

Church membership has always been a part of my life. As I grew into an adult, my weekly attendance at church was inherent, to say the least. Needless to say, I considered myself to be very much a "church girl." In my forty plus years of life, there has never been a time I have not been in church.

I grew up in what could be considered the neighborhood church. It was within walking distance of the apartments we lived in and even shared the same name. On Sundays when my mother had to work, I would walk to attend morning worship service. There was a convenient path behind the apartment building across from ours, or I could go down the hill and cut through the lot of the neighborhood store to get to church. I remember one particular Sunday, my mother was working and I didn't want to miss church because I was usually a part of the program for youth Sunday. My outfit choice for the day was a striped top and a plaid skirt. The colors were relatively close so it worked for me even though that mix of patterns may not have been as popular in the early eighties. After service, a lady in the church made a comment to me that she knew my mother had to be working that day because she could tell I dressed myself. I suppose I was a bit too fashion forward for her. Nonetheless, I made it to church. In addition to my consistent Sunday attendance which included singing in the choir and ushering, there was also regular bible study attendance and youth trips or activities.

Even as a late teen and young adult, I was sure to attend Sunday morning service regardless of where I had been the night before. There were times when me and my best friend would have been out late the night before so we would barely make it to church. Fortunately, there was a back entrance that allowed us to enter the sanctuary near the musicians and slide right into our seats on the choir stand. Our goal was just to get there, hopefully before the message (depending on who was preaching), and definitely before the benediction.

In my early twenties, I begin to desire more spiritual growth, so I left the church I grew up in and joined a non-denominational church. My mother was not in favor of this decision. However, as a new "grown-up" I exercised my right to make my own decisions. The congregation was small and the building was a storefront which I believe was difficult for her to embrace because it was different from what she had known. She was so against it, that she would sometimes say, "Y'all still having church up there in that 'lil building?" You would have to have known her to know that when she did speak, it was what she felt and thought, so it was best to not be easily offended if you wanted her truth. I would answer, "Yes, we are," and keep it moving.

The transition to another church turned my servitude up a notch. I served wherever needed and if you've ever been in a small church, you know that can mean wearing many hats. For me it was the praise team, youth ministry, media ministry and helping with clerical duties as needed.

My love for church evolved into me traveling evenings and weekends for additional services, conferences and workshops. This level of activity felt very natural for me as a "church girl." I wanted to continue to grow spiritually, and I began to follow a leader and ministry that I felt destined to be connected to. The ministry was not local so I traveled frequently for services and events. I was open to instructions for what was next, and I eventually relocated to be closer. Consequently, I became a founding member of a new church. The timeline was about six months from the initial meeting to our first Sunday service. There was much work to be done in preparation for the first service, but we all worked in eager anticipation and with a deep love for our church. Since it was a new church, many of us served in multiple areas. I served as administrative and office staff, a Youth Ministry Leader and a choir member.

Though the areas of service may have changed over time, the level of commitment did not. I recall a small window of time when I was at the church daily; yes, seven days a week. My days consisted of prayer sessions, choir rehearsal, Bible study, administrative work and special events or services. Outside of work, church related activities were a priority. This was normal behavior for me and my circle supported it, so nothing was questioned. I viewed service and attendance as indicators to depth of relationship, and mistakenly thought this was a requirement for a deeper relationship with God. I felt that I was well, and thought I was thriving until my spiritual health began to fail.

CHAPTER 3

PRONE TO INJURY

The practice or lifestyle of "being" was lacking for me because the focus was always "doing." What does it look like to be more concerned with doing church? In short, it's having a lack of understanding of God's love, goodness and grace. Church culture had become my way of life. I not only knew what to do, I also looked the part. The truth is, I mastered doing church so much that my routines and patterns overshadowed me functioning as a member of the body of Christ. Even though my religious practices left me lacking in other areas, they didn't seem wrong to me because I was effective in my local church. I was in a "perfect church" box, and I had a distorted view of the world outside of my box.

God has a unique way of giving me a nudge to get my attention. I had a roommate that attended the same church, and we shared a vanity space in our home. We were both in the mirror grooming before we left for a church service and I heard the words, "Playing dress up." It was an audible interruption of my thoughts, and it was so profound that I glanced at my roommate to see if she may have heard it also. She was visibly unbothered, so we continued our routine.

I think I mentally attached what I heard as a reference to wardrobe and not character. We were young women and our standard church attire was skirt suits, pantyhose, and heels. Even with what I heard, I was unaware that the course of my life was about to change. It was in the midst of this heightened level of service that I received a huge blow that would inflict injury and uncover the truth about my current condition. As I think back to that time, it reminds me of the warning you get from someone that loves you when you're repeatedly doing something dangerous: "Keep on... you're going to get hurt!"

Church hurt was not in my vocabulary and I had no point of reference for it. From experiences shared in prior chapters, you may agree that I had a strong affection for church. Though church hurt is what it's called, the entire church did not hurt me. The source of my hurt came from being put out and excommunicated from a local church I served in for almost ten years.

While I know church hurt is just as much a controversial topic as church attendance, I don't debate it. I was completely blindsided by my experience, so I'll share my stance. The primary reason I don't debate the subject is because I believe that no one has the right to tell another person what hurts them, especially from an inexperienced and judgmental place. There are many things that I have not experienced that are sensitive and hurtful areas for those that have. Therefore, I am careful in not interpreting their feelings about a specific experience. I am also a firm believer that what may have once hindered us doesn't have to cripple us, which seems to be the main issue for most people that debate church hurt. The topic is taboo for many because once the hurt is inflicted, they have a personal vendetta with the church as a whole, while never fully healing or confronting the individuals that caused the hurt.

My experience with church hurt happened at a time when I was recovering from an emergency surgery. I was thirty-five years old, and this was my very first hospital stay and first surgery. Fortunately, the surgery was a one-time fix with a two-week recovery period. However, the underlying issues that were discovered after this experience with church would take years to heal. There were layers that had to be undone from years of practiced behaviors.

I now know that it was with purpose far greater than I could wrap my mind around at the time. As I've grown older, I've realized that everything bad that happens to you, is not bad for you. I'm grateful that it happened, and it initiated a needed healing process for me.

CHAPTER 4

THE WOUND

In 2015, I suffered a very bad fall. I was leaving from visiting someone's home, lost my balance and fell while walking down three uneven, concrete steps. Fortunately, there were no broken bones; only scrapes, bruises and intense pain. My left shin took the brunt of the blow from the fall. I had on pantyhose that had to be torn off because I was bleeding and I could feel the sting of the abrasion. When I got home, I cleaned the abrasion and applied a topical skin treatment to the area. The next day, I noticed some swelling, so I elevated my leg and applied ice. After doctoring on it and monitoring it myself for a few days, it didn't seem to be healing well.

I have a friend who worked as a wound nurse at the time so I spoke with her about the swelling to see if she had any suggestions for recovery. She requested to see the area, and informed me that I didn't have an abrasion, but I instead had a wound. Wounds are more serious because most of their damage cannot be seen on the surface.

> *wound (noun): an injury to living tissue caused by a cut, blow, or other impact, typically one in which the skin is cut or broken.*

For the next several weeks, she treated the area for me. This included multiple trips for dressing changes, cleaning and applying medicine to the wound and compression wrapping from my knee to my toes to deal with the swelling. This was much more than I anticipated for what I assumed was a really bad scrape. I was grateful for her care and expertise because she provided treatment until the wound healed. I have a permanent scar that has become less noticeable over time, but serves as a reminder of the pain of that moment and the tedious process of healing.

My immediate response to that injury was similar to how I responded when I was excommunicated from my former church. The initial sting and shock caused me to respond like it was an abrasion, because I was unaware of the depth of the damage. As life changing as it was, I was not going to be too moved; so I thought, because that's what is expected from a strong person.

I'm one of those that's typically labeled as a strong person; not always because I want to be, but as a natural leader that's often where I land. When you're a person that's known to exude strength, it's sometimes hard to acknowledge pain. For the most part, I have an even keeled temperament and I don't appear to be greatly moved by many things. Other than dramatic facial expressions that happen unintentionally, my reactions are usually minimal. Those that have witnessed my extreme response to music or certain recording artists are usually shocked because it's a polar opposite of my regular demeanor.

Immediately after my church hurt experience, I had a few conversations about the initial shock and anger, but had not dealt with what was beneath the surface. It was an altar call that I did not want to participate in that helped me identify that I had a wound, not an abrasion. That altar call helped me identify the wound as church hurt. Just as I didn't know the depth of the hurt, I was unaware of what the healing process would require, but I'm grateful the Great Physician did.

One of the things I learned from my leg injury was that movement and activity is required at some point during the healing process. It aides the blood flow and the blood flow is necessary for healing. Movement was challenging because instead of resting and elevating my leg for the swelling, I wore restrictive compression wrap. I still had to move around and apply pressure to my leg even though the wrap was uncomfortable.

The process of healing from church hurt also required movement and activity. Of course, I had a home remedy for this as well. It included keeping a "safe" distance when I attended church and purposely fellowshipping in a large congregation so I wouldn't have to get involved. This worked for a while until it was time to apply more pressure to increase the blood flow and aide the healing process. The movement needed required me joining a church again. My plan was shattered because I only desired to be a member by name and attendance. I had no desire to be active in church and definitely did not want to develop new relationships with "church people." It was clear that I was going to have to be uncomfortable to get through this process.

There were a number of lessons I needed to learn. One of the main lessons was to have realistic expectations of people that attend church, whether leaders or members. We are not elite. We simply make the decision to regularly fellowship with a body of believers at a set location. Regardless of how charismatic the services are, how grand the building or how phenomenal the teaching and preaching is, attending church alone does not change us. My practical statement to remind me that Christians are not in a class of their own is this: "The people that show up at church on Sundays are the same people that show up to work on Monday with their flaws, attitudes, and masks." In other words, entering the church building does not change us. Repentance brings about change, and that change should be evident daily; not only during church services. I had to shatter pretentious expectations to embrace truth for myself while extending grace to accept it in others. I no longer expect perfection from myself or others.

Being in church again did not remove any damage from the wound, it was an essential step towards my healing. Just like any other wound, this one was not

> *A scar is an area of fibrous tissue that replaces normal skin after an injury. Scars result from the biological process of wound repair in the skin, as well as in other organs and tissues of the body. Thus, scarring is a natural part of the healing process. With the exception of very minor lesions, every wound (e.g., after accident, disease, or surgery) results in some degree of scarring.*

without scarring. The scar was visible evidence of the wound, but the depth of the wound caused pain to surface in other areas of my life. As they were exposed, I had to address the layers to my healing process. How I handled relationships is an area where some of the damaged layers were exposed. When my time at my previous church ended, my relationships were impacted. Some relationships that I thought would be lifelong shifted, declined and ended. This caused me to view other relationships through a different lens; a lens of rejection and abandonment.

Because of this obscured view, things that may have been overlooked or accepted in the past were more sensitive to me. I found myself responding to emotional triggers in relationships. In some cases, my responses resulted in breaches and severed relationships. I felt I had to protect myself once I encountered any offense, big or small, causing me to exit first. I eventually had to acknowledge that I was acting out of fear of abandonment in relationships. I would act out how I felt rather than having a discussion about my feelings.

Realizing that I could soon end up losing quality relationships if this continued to be my response, I sought out a remedy. Like many relationships, the remedy I needed was communication. If there is value in the relationship, it's worth having the hard conversations. Those are the conversations where you are open enough to receive the truth about any hurt or offense you have caused and expressing areas where you've been hurt or offended. As difficult as honest conversation and confrontation can be, they are both vital to healthy relationships. After recognizing and acknowledging my actions, I am now more self-aware and willing to have hard conversations for the sake of the relationship.

When there has been a breach in relationship, moving forward requires me to own what I contribute, what I accept, and what I allow from others. I am now more willing to express an area of concern before making a transition in relationships. This is an ongoing healing process for me. This is not always easy and I'm still growing in this area. Each relationship is unique and I've learned that there are some situations that I will have to go through, some I will grow through, and some I'll still have to let go.

CHAPTER 5

THE INFECTION

Infections may not immediately have outward symptoms but they can spread and cause great damage the longer they are untreated. My infection was bondage; emotionally, mentally and spiritually. At some point in my journey, I adopted the mindset that the practices and beliefs endorsed and upheld by me and those I associated with were THE WAY. If others were outside of that circle, or if they did not attend or associate with church, their relationship with God was

> *bondage: The state of being a slave (A person who is excessively dependent upon or controlled by something).*

questionable to me and honestly, I kept my distance.

Passing judgement based on church attendance, and the appearance and actions of others caused me to hold tight to those that fit my expected mold or were in my community. Ironically, many from the same group I held tight to shunned me when I was no longer a part of the community. The truth is, I had done the same thing to others, not realizing it was a manifestation of the infection of bondage. I had an occurrence where I saw people that I knew from church, but purposely did not speak to them because of who they were and things I knew they had done. This behavior of ignoring or avoiding people was common for me before making a serious commitment to Christ, but this incident occurred while I was deeply serving in church. I felt justified in my wrong behavior because I focused on what I felt they did wrong. I was so sick! Symptoms of infection were surfacing and I didn't even realize it. I have since seen those individuals again on a few occasions. While I can't erase or undo the moment from the past, I now choose to greet them, respond appropriately and extend kindness.

I did not know that I was bound mentally. When I embraced the transition from my previous church, areas of bondage began to peel away in layers. Bondage screams loudest in the midst of freedom so my mental bondages were being challenged. While tunnel vision is beneficial for focus, tunnel thinking is detrimental to growth. I developed a mental box that I placed "church people" in, and it worked in my previous environment. The majority of the people I had close relationships with fit perfectly in that box and I concluded that they were safe. Each moment of freedom I experienced as I moved forward opened my eyes to what I never looked at as bondage.

My way of life was if church was going on, I had to be there because I was supposed to be. Missing services was allowed only under extreme circumstances so it rarely happened. After the excommunication, I moved back to my home town and moved in with family. I was in the beginning stages of healing from church hurt and though I didn't want to join a church, I would attend services with my family. This included Sunday morning worship services and Bible study on Wednesday nights. I recall a Wednesday evening when they decided not to go to Bible study and I questioned why they weren't going. They were simply tired and opted to stay home. This was normal for them, but abnormal for me. I had to wrap my mind around the thought of not going to church and not having to report in, get permission or explain why to anyone. Moments like that made me aware that much of my bondage was self-inflicted, but it was reinforced by my chosen community that believed and functioned the same way.

As a young Christian, I made choices that helped me focus on my spiritual growth, but I would later learn that many of my decisions caused me to make my world small. I implemented what I thought were necessary lifestyle restrictions because I grew up in a church that didn't appear to place emphasis on lifestyle. In my early twenties, I stopped listening to any music that was not labeled as

Christian or gospel music. I love music, so this was big for me. Everything I listened to wasn't positive and I didn't want anything to hinder my spiritual growth. I knew I was serious when I parted ways with the cassette, Black Reign, by Queen Latifah. It felt like a big sacrifice because that was my jam! I wanted a license plate with the words "Black Reign" on it made for the front of my red Ford Escort and I was going to get one of those crowns from the beauty supply store to sit in my back window. Yep, I was all in. Even though I didn't get the plate and crown, that cassette was definitely my riding music. To feed my love for music, I would listen to various styles of Christian or gospel music including traditional, southern gospel, contemporary, rap, praise & worship and anything else I could find that seemed to fit the genre. I had an extensive Christian and Gospel music collection and enjoyed sharing music finds with others.

After moving back home, I began to form new relationships, and many of them were with musicians, singers and others that shared a love for music. While spending more time with them, I learned they listened to, played and created music beyond the limits of a genre. They were very confident in their spirituality, their relationship with God, committed to their gifts and callings, and purposeful about enjoying life. Honestly, these relationships were eye opening for me. Each new experience made me feel like a butterfly peeking out of its cocoon wondering if it was really safe to come out. Could you really enjoy life at this level as a Christian? It was in these new relationships, developed beyond the hurt, that the antibiotic in the form of love would be administered to me from unexpected sources.

On another occasion, I attended a luau themed event hosted offsite by the single's ministry of a local church. It was an opportunity for me to meet some new people and reconnect with those I haven't seen or spoken with in years. Attendees were dressed for the theme, and there was music, food, games and laughter; a classic combination for a great time. Towards the end of the event, they started playing line dance songs and the dancers jumped right up to enjoy their favorite line dances. Dancing is a natural response for many when they hear music, but I was confused. The "church people" were dancing at the church event. Was this allowed? Was this right? I was so confused! I wasn't against dancing because I love attending dance exercise classes, which I considered an appropriate setting for dancing; but not at a church event. So, I did the good "church girl" thing and sat on the sidelines as if I didn't enjoy dancing. Honestly outside of exercise, it had been so long I'm sure I didn't know the moves anyway. I'm happy to say that I overcame this mental bondage. My favorite form of exercise is dance, specifically Zumba®. The freedom to dance felt so good that I became a licensed instructor to teach Zumba® classes. I am also happy to say that whenever time and opportunity allows, I will jump on the dance floor now. As bondage is released, freedom is embraced.

The ability to open your mind to embrace the differences of another is not only liberating, but it immediately expands your world. Though not impossible, a mindset is difficult to change. I was challenged each time I met new people that

I would have previously shunned because they lived outside of my "church people" box; especially those that were professed Christians. Yes, I said Christians. Why? Because I equated Christians to the "church people" that were supposed to fit in my mental box. Anything outside of that was questionable to me. Am I saying Christians shouldn't have standards and boundaries? That's not what I am saying at all. What I am saying, however, is that while you maintain your moral standards and enforce your boundaries, know that God has placed treasures in vessels that your tunnel thinking would otherwise discard.

I'm so grateful that God is so concerned about my wholeness and health that I'm continually presented with moments to expose the infected areas of my life, allow His blood to flow to those areas, and prompt healing to continue.

CHAPTER 6

THE HANDICAP

Many handicaps are evident because of their crippling effect. I became so acclimated to my handicap that I didn't realize it was there, and I'm not certain who else could notice.

handicap: a circumstance that makes progress or success difficult

My handicap was a mistaken identity. You may have gathered from the previous chapters that my life and my identity were consumed with church. I remember being thirty-five years old, excommunicated from a local church and questioning, "Who am I now?"

My identity was based on performance and relationships. My value and worth came from feeling needed by others and feeling important to the ministries I served in. Religious routines had become my comfort zones, though they were not without challenges.

When I no longer wore the veil of doing good for church, I had to deal with other areas in my life that I allowed to deteriorate. My personal finances were one of those areas. Financially, I suffered from what I describe as unrestrained ignorance. You're ignorant in an area because you lack knowledge but when you function as if you know and don't seek help, I call that unrestrained ignorance. I didn't have good financial habits because I hadn't been taught, and choosing not to seek the knowledge even though I had financial responsibilities kept my ignorance unrestrained. I have always been a giver and once I learned the principle and experienced the benefits of tithing, giving in church happened without question. While I had an excellent giving record at church, I had poor credit and owed the IRS thousands of dollars. I had a good reputation at church but a bad name with creditors. Functioning with a mistaken identity had me focusing on one-sided righteousness. True spiritual development should also enhance your personal life.

Unrestrained ignorance then resulted in unrestrained pride. The pride surfaced from me being ashamed of admitting what I didn't know and instead focusing on an area of my life that appeared more appealing. To move past this cycle, I had to evaluate my actions, be vocal about my condition (ask for help), get the knowledge and change my behaviors. Fortunately, I did the work to rectify those financial issues and I'm still able to give as I desire.

I also needed to change my approach to ministry. Once I was in a different church, I had to discover who Tammy was outside of working or serving someone else. Like clockwork, I knew how and when to show up in my previous church. The desire to build the vision I was attached to was a priority and the driving force for my showing up without fail. I didn't fully realize it at the time, but I was serving in preparation for what was ahead for me. Am I saying I am beyond serving others? Absolutely not. I still serve others and enjoy doing it. Fortunately, I am now in a place where I am willing to apply weight to areas that are now healed and strengthened. In other words, I want to apply the knowledge I gain while serving to build the Kingdom in my place of righteousness and responsibility. I am able to walk in my light and not in another's shadow. I am grateful for the wisdom that's gained in the shadow of others, but the application of that wisdom enhances your light of individuality.

Showing up in the areas of your strengths and responsibility is difficult when you become accustomed to working on what others have validated in you. This area of growth also challenged my trust in God. I have been in leadership in ministry for several years, and every endeavor that I led was attached to someone else's vision as an extension of their established work. When God began to instruct me and reveal vision to me, I struggled with questioning if He could carry those things out through me. My issue wasn't with God's ability, it was with wondering whether or not I was capable to establish and lead something on my own.

We sometimes have an arsenal of excuses as to why we can't do what God is showing us or why He should choose someone else over us. We don't realize that when we let these excuses win, we are shortening our reach or depending solely on our physical sight and not experiencing God's vision or His expected end for our lives. I remember driving one day and pondering some heart desires for my future concerning ministry. Even in my thoughts, I began to question if that was really for me. My thoughts were interrupted by the question, "Why are you trying to make Me a respecter of persons?" This was God's way of reminding me that because I've seen Him do these things for others, then why not me.

There is strength in using my voice and embracing individuality, knowing that while I'll forever be learning and growing, I don't have to seek approval to be who God has designed me to be. I've learned ultimate freedom is found in discovering and becoming who God has called you to be. As you discover your place of righteousness, you may find that it's bigger than a church building or a denomination. You may also discover resources to help you progress in unlikely people and places.

God is faithful to complete what He began in us. Knowing that, I had to move from a mindset of serving God for His goodness to someone else while shying away from His goodness to me. He's a good, good Father. When we show up in the places God calls us to, His abundant and amazing grace meets us there and His ability overrides our capability.

CHAPTER 7

NOT JUST A "CHURCH GIRL"

It feels like I've been on an accelerated track of learning and growth the past several years. Prior to being hurt, I know I functioned as one that so easily pointed out another's faults as if I didn't have any, as if their faults were bigger than mine or even worse; as if we all don't need God's grace daily. While I acknowledge that I had an infection (bondage), I also acknowledge that I spread infection each time I chose to talk instead of pray; turn away instead of come close; judge instead of trying to understand. This is detrimental to the body of Christ and I was hindering myself. I can't heal or grow if I'm not honest about me. I can't be honest about me if I choose to focus more on others. Until I was hurt, I would have defended how well I was. However, I needed both the rest and recovery that followed the hurt.

I don't share my experience from a place of being a victim. I'm by no means a victim. I embrace every experience as necessary for my journey. In an honest reflection, many of the self-imposed, but crowd supported restrictions I lived by were helpful for me at the time. I'm certain my "all in" commitment and behaviors protected me from me and established boundaries that I still appreciate.

I still very much love the church and remain an advocate for the necessity of it, but I'm no longer just a "church girl." That persona had me in self-inflicted bondage in hopes of gaining approval and love from a Father that already loved me. This only allowed me to gain temporary fanfare from people. I'm sure part of my behavior was a manifestation of being from a single parent home and not knowing the pureness of a father's love. My father was murdered when I was six years old, and although my oldest brother filled in the gaps where he could, he could never be my father.

God loves me simply because I belong to Him. I now embrace that God loved me before I ever made the decision to live for Him. (Romans 5:8) His love is a consistent and unconditional love, greater than any we've ever known, not fickle and conditional like man's. *I know I am loved* and can extend love to others.

How can I say that I'm healed? To acknowledge healing we must first admit that there was a condition and a need. I've experienced the symptoms of my wound, infection and handicap. I have the scars and remember pivotal moments during the recovery. I admit that the recovery is an ongoing process and I have progressed further than I anticipated.

I've learned authentic forgiveness. Not just issuing an apology as a temporary bandage, but genuine forgiveness and reconciliation. Being able to continue in relationships, even if on different terms, beyond known offenses is a by-product of forgiveness. *I know I am forgiven* and I can extend forgiveness to others.

I now approach life from a holistic perspective. I no longer neglect other areas of my life and place issues behind a wall of religious practices. Going to church did not grant me access to a magic wand that fixed my life. I needed to live better for me, which is an inward work first. *I know that I am whole* and I desire to share the journey to wholeness with others.

Like many, as a child I dreamed big for my life, but at some point, I became content in just being a part of someone else's dream. While I'm in the midst of things yet unfolding in my life, I've had many experiences beyond what I imagined. God's desire for us is to have life; abundantly! (John 10:10) Beyond existing, I LIVE now. Living for Him is not bondage. Yes, there are standards, but standards are not chains. *I know I have freedom* to live an abundant LIFE and I want to share that with others.

Above all, I've learned to no longer attempt to box God in; it's impossible to do so. He is omniscient, omnipotent and omnipresent. His wisdom is infinite and His greatness is unsearchable. Church hurt was not a death sentence for me. It was a catalyst. My heart is healed and my life is open. Nothing is impossible with God.

What initially felt like one of the worst things to happen to me truly became one of the best things that happened. Beyond my knowledge at the time, it was the pruning I needed to continue to bloom. My life's story is great, and it is still unfolding. My experiences have worked for my good.

CHAPTER 8

YOUR PERSONAL CHECK UP

Many people attending church have suffered through hurts they never sought help for. They are serving and smiling through pain. They appear to be well, but there is a wound, an infection or a handicap that they are covering. Without healing, they are very likely inflicting wounds and spreading infection to others. Unfortunately, the place and the people wherewith we should know freedom at its best is where many suffer the strongest bondage.

I hope your desire to read this book was not from a place of finding fault or pointing fingers at an individual or the church. You can see by now, that's not my heart, intent or desire. In the early stages of processing what happened to me, God helped me to change my perspective so I could completely forgive and move forward. I had to understand that everything that happens to me, is not always about me. In other words, a person's actions can be a result of where they are mentally or emotionally and you are on the receiving end because of the nature of your relationship with them. Does this excuse their actions? Of course not. However, the same grace that covers me and my actions is present for them.

I shared how I exhibited toxic behavior while active in church and I was very likely the source of offense and hurt to others. It took my own experience to shift my mindset and perspective, resulting in changed behavior. So, where are you? Are you a blessed and highly favored hypocrite? It sounds harsh, but that's what I was. The truth is, many are toxic and hide behind religious practices to justify behaviors.

If that's you, your wound is oozing, your infection is spreading and your handicap is visible. I invite you to join me in acknowledging and standing in truth.

I know from experience there is healing and abundant LIFE beyond church hurt. We seek help and successfully move forward from so many other physical and emotional injuries; this one can be remedied also. You may be in a place where you feel stuck in offense, you have unidentified or unresolved issues, or you may be in a place of spreading offense and hurt to others. My prayer is that you too move beyond where you are and walk in the freedom to begin a new course.

Make love a priority. Filter your responses through compassion and consideration. Don't be so far removed from your past that you have no empathy for another's current condition. Become teachers of what you have mastered instead of judging those in the same struggles. I believe we can truly function as a body, fitly joined together with every joint supplying.

The following questions may help you reflect, identify where you are, and begin to move forward. Take time to journal your responses, thoughts and the instructions you hear from God.

- If you attend and you're active in a local church, what is your WHY?

- If you don't or no longer attend church, what is your WHY?

- Do you feel you have been hurt by people in church?

- Do you have unresolved issues with anyone or breached relationships?

- Have you forgiven those that inflicted offense or injury to you?

- Have you reflected on your own decisions or actions and asked forgiveness of those you may have offended or injured?

- Are you withholding your gifts as a result of an offense or injury received in church?

> Are areas of your life suffering because you're masking issues or dealing with unrestrained ignorance and pride?

> Have you sincerely prayed and asked God what's next for you?

Once God reveals what's next for you, be willing to obey His instructions. He may have you initiate a conversation, issue an apology or completely change your environment and routine. Your next step may look very different than what you are accustomed to. Embrace new places and people; be open to where God leads you. You can make an impact both inside and outside of a local church. Focus on being whole so you can function wherever you are needed. You need to be whole for you above all else. However, every life directly attached to yours needs you to be well, the world needs you, and we, the body of Christ, need you.

Trust God's guidance. He knows your end and He's ordering your steps to get you there. Just like mine, your experiences are working for your good. He came that you may have life and have it MORE ABUNDANTLY. So live healed, live whole, and live LOVED!

ABOUT THE AUTHOR

Tammy Carpenter discovered her love for equipping and empowering others over 20 years ago when she began her career as a Software Trainer & Consultant. Her profession connects with her passion and her faith as she aspires to share truths to inspire.

Tammy is a published author of several books, a licensed Minister and the passionate Founder of the non-profit organization, enLife, which offers programs and services to help women succeed through transition. Tammy helps other authors bring life to their vision by offering consulting and formatting services through her business, Effectual Concepts.

Tammy is certain that one of her assignments is to help women celebrate and share their journeys. Using her brand name, Simply Tammy, she launched the Women Who Win vodcast where she hosts interviews with women who are willing to be transparent about their journey with the aim to encourage and inspire others.

Whether through a message, conversation, forum, or her inspirational products, Tammy desires to encourage others to LIVE and LOVE. She is most grateful to God for transforming her life and that gratitude fuels her desire to share God's love with others.

To contact the author or purchase additional books, visit
www.simplytammy.com